HOW TO DEVELOP YOUR ENTREPRENEURIAL MIND

GBENGA SHOWUNMI

HOW TO DEVELOP YOUR ENTREPRENEURIAL MIND

Copyright © 2017 by **Gbenga Showunmi**

ISBN: 978-1-944652-47-0

Cornerstone Publishing
A Division Cornerstone Creativity Group LLC
Phone: +1(516) 547-4999
info@thecornerstonepublishers.com
www.thecornerstonepublishers.com

To order this book or for speaking engagement:
Gbenga Showunmi
Focuspint Business Network
info@gbengashowunmi.com
Phone: +1 (516) 547-4999
www.gbengashowunmi.com

This publication may not be reproduced, stored in a retrieval system, or transmitted in whole or in part, in any form or by any means, electronic, mechanical, photocopying, recording, or otherwise, without the prior written permission of the publisher.
All rights reserved.

Printed in United States of America

CONTENTS

About the Author..7
Introduction..9
1. So Why Should You Consider Becoming an Entrepreneur?..17
2. Developing a Positive Attitude...............................25
3. The Motivation Equation...31
4. How to Generate a Steady Stream of Ideas and Tapping Into Your Creative Side...........................37
5. How to Be More Open and Aware of Opportunities...41
6. Be Very Competitive..47
7. Take Advantage of Your Resources.......................51
8. Resilience in entrepreneur...55
9. How to Wear the Entrepreneurial Hat (You're More Than a Manager)..59
10. How to Share Your Business Vision.......................63
11. How to Be a Problem Solver...................................69
12. Entrepreneurial Mind Means Being Willing To Take Risks..73
13. Entrepreneurs Always Learn and Improve..........77
14. Entrepreneurs Know Their Strengths and Weaknesses..81
15. Living the Entrepreneur Lifestyle..........................85

Bonus Setting Your Business Goals............................91

Thus says the Lord, your Redeemer, The Holy One of Israel: "I am the Lord your God, Who teaches you to profit, Who leads you by the way you should go.

ISAIAH 48:17

ABOUT THE AUTHOR

Gbenga Showunmi is an insightful speaker, book-publishing strategist and business startup coach. He is the senior pastor of Destinystar International Church, Houston Texas and CEO of Cornerstone Creativity Group LLC and Cornerstone Publishing. He has helped lots of businesses take off from scratch and many see him as a leading authority in raising and shaping new entrepreneurial minds.

As a 3rd generation successful and award winning entrepreneur, Gbenga is the visionary behind Focuspoint Business Network (FBN), a network for mentoring and helping businesses to reach their full potential through referrals. The focus is on building a community of business minded men and women to network, renew, and activate their entrepreneurial ideas.

Gbenga Showunmi is a prolific writer and author of 15 best selling books, including

In Pursuit of Greatness, The Prosperity Mindset, Moving Forward in the Storm, Your Supernatural Inheritance, and Prophetic Prayer for Divine Intervention.

Gbenga is a graduate of Masters of Divinity from Oral Roberts University, Tulsa Oklahoma. His life's goal is to help people move toward achieving God's purposes for their lives. He is a loving husband and proud father of 3 destiny children. He and his family reside in Houston Texas.

INTRODUCTION

Entrepreneurship is the art of stepping into and operating in the business world as a value creator, offering goods and services and solving people's problems.

While business is a venture to provide valuable product and services with the intent to make profit.

What Is An Entrepreneurial Mind And Why Is It Important?

There is a difference between being a business owner and being an entrepreneur. There are millions of business owners around the globe. There are much fewer entrepreneurs.

Why?

Being an entrepreneur requires a certain mindset. It is a mind that many are born with. You've met and likely heard of people who have always had one business idea or another and acted on them regularly. From the time they were small children they were out making money and starting businesses.

These people were born with an entrepreneurial mind. They are innovative, action takers who aren't afraid to make mistakes. They're also often very skilled at getting people to buy into their vision.

As a business owner, or aspiring business owner, you can benefit from this entrepreneurial mind. You can grow your business well beyond your original plan and have a lot of fun along the way.

You see, entrepreneurs are:
1. Positive
2. Motivated
3. Innovative and creative
4. Open minded
5. Resourceful
6. Visionaries
7. Delegators
8. Problem solvers
9. Risk takers
10. Lifelong learners

11. Self aware
12. Balanced
13. Resilience
14. Competitive

These are the 14 key ingredients of an entrepreneurial mind. Taking a look at the list, it is not hard to see why an entrepreneurial mind is so powerful in business. Chances are you already possess some of these key attributes. You may possess many of them in varying degrees.

For example, some days you're confident to take calculated risks. Other days, not so much. This book is designed to help you cultivate all of these attributes and it is designed to help you develop an entrepreneurial mind.

To put it quite simply, an entrepreneurial mind gives you the power to:
- Recognize and capitalize on opportunities
- Operate from a place of confidence and courage
- Take calculated risks
- Stay passionate and enthusiastic
- Connect with, and lead, people who can

help your business thrive and prosper
- Tap into the courage and determination it takes to make it through challenges
- Learn from, and capitalize on mistakes.
- Make an impact on your audience and in your world

How to Use This Book

This book is designed to help you develop and embrace an entrepreneurial spirit and mind. Use the information provided in these pages to fine tune the areas where your entrepreneurial mind may need a little work. It's okay if you need to work on all areas. Mindset is learned, not ingrained in your DNA. The path of business ownership and creation is one filled with continuous learning, adaptation, and growth. Developing your entrepreneurial mind is part of that path and process.

There are two potential approaches to using this book.

The first is to read it through cover to cover. Then go back and review and work on the areas where you need the most improvement. Or work on the areas that inspire you. This is the appropriate approach if you like to read material and think on it before you take action. However, you may want to keep a notebook handy when you are reading so you can jot down any thoughts or notes.

The second approach is to read the book and take action as you work your way through it. For example, if you are inspired and motivated to start working on your ability to visualize then take action on that inspiration.

Of course you can always take a combined approach. Take notes on some items and action on others!

In this book you'll learn:
- How to get and stay positive.
- How to get and stay motivated.
- How to generate a steady stream of ideas and tapping into your creative side.
- How to be more open and aware of opportunities.
- How to consistently take advantage of your resources.
- How to wear the entrepreneurial hat (you're more than a manager).

- How to share your business vision.
- How to be a problem solver.
- How to take more risk and confidently.
- How to create a plan for lifelong learning and self improvement.
- How to become more self aware - know your strengths and weaknesses.

How to live a balanced life

Let's get started with a little quiz - Do you have an entrepreneurial mind?

Do You Have an Entrepreneurial mind - A Quiz

Simply answer yes or no to the following 15 questions. The more yes answers you have, the stronger your entrepreneurial mind.

- I passionately seek new opportunities.
- I am focused and determined.
- I effectively tune out negative people, comments and thoughts.
- I am confident in business.
- I take inspired action and make decisions quickly
- I regularly see opportunities around me
- I have many fulfilling business relationships
- I enjoy sharing my vision with others

- I take advantage of my resources
- I am creative and/or enjoy creative problem solving.
- I am comfortable making tough choices.
- I know my strengths and weaknesses
- I trust my gut.
- I know when something isn't working for me.
- I'm not afraid to fail.

How many Yes answers did you have? ____ Don't worry if you have zero yes answers. That's what this book is for! Take the quiz at the end of the book, after you have worked on the entrepreneurial attributes discussed in this book, go back and take the quiz again.

For now, let's move onto the first and perhaps most important chapter in this book.

Chapter One

SO WHY SHOULD YOU CONSIDER BECOMING AN ENTREPRENEUR?

A recent survey found that more than 70% of people want to be some sort of entrepreneur. Becoming an entrepreneur is a sought after job for many reasons, including pride, purpose and possibly money. Starting and running your own business on a day to day basis is no easy task, but it is one that is truly worth the effort.

There are many reasons why you should consider taking that giant step and creating your own business. Here are just a few of them:

1. **Autonomy:** running your own business allows you to be in charge of your own

destiny. It also helps you to avoid getting stuck in the "daily grind" or the "rat race". For many people running their own business lets them have a career that is self-sustaining.

2. **Opportunity:** Being an entrepreneur opens up a whole new world of opportunity for you. You will have the opportunity to do anything that you want in life. This means you can choose to spend your life changing the world for the better, or you can live the type of life you want. Few other career choices can offer this kind of opportunity.

3. **Impact:** Many people who work for other companies truly want to work hard and help that company to succeed, but few are actually able to have such an impact. When you run your own business everything you do will directly impact the company, which can be very rewarding.

4. **Freedom:** this is the answer most people will give if you ask them why they want to become an entrepreneur. For many people the idea of doing what they want and how they want to do is the most compelling

reason to take the risk and run their own business. It is true- having freedom in life and career does make a huge difference!

5. **Responsibility:** when you run your own business you have the ability to be responsible to society and operate your business the way that you feel it should be run. This is especially true if you have the desire to help others or the world in general. If you work for someone else you may not be able to improve the world the way you want to, but if you are the boss you can.

6. **Being your Own Boss:** this is another common answer for why many people want to become entrepreneurs. If you are your own boss you can do things your way. You can make your own decisions, take your own risks and decide your own fate.

7. **Time and Family:** depending on your specific goals in life, becoming an entrepreneur could give you the freedom of time and allow you to spend more of it with your family.

8. **Creating a Legacy:** if the idea of forging a lasting legacy is important to you then few other careers give you the opportunity to do so like operating your own business.

9. **Accomplishment:** if you have specific goals that you would like to accomplish in your life running your own business could help you to do so.

10. **Control:** for a lot of business owners the sense of security that comes with the ability to control your own work is a major reason to become an entrepreneur.

Some Skills That Will Help You to Become a Successful Entrepreneur

- Focus: running your own business requires dealing with any number of factors on any given day. Successful business owners are able to pinpoint their focus onto accomplishing specific tasks and goals at specific times.
- Resilience: it is a skill to be able to weather the various ups and downs of business without allowing them to destroy your focus. Truly successful entrepreneurs are

able to continue traveling down the path of success even when the future looks bleak.
- Management Skills: a successful company requires the right people and successful business owners need to know how to properly manage these people.
- Long Term Vision: while it is easy to focus on what the company needs to do in the next several days or weeks to be successful, truly exceptional entrepreneurs (the ones who see real success in their business ventures) are able to plan years ahead of time.
- Salesmanship: regardless of what type of company you are running, you need to be able to sell your vision to others in order to become successful. Entrepreneurs need to have great salesmanship skills whether they want to or not.
- Self-reliance: this is one of the most important skills any entrepreneur can possess. It is vital for a business owner to trust that they can depend on themselves.
- Self-reflection: the ability to pause, reflect and learn is a very valuable skill for the business owner. Entrepreneurs must be able to learn from their mistakes and reflect

upon what they have learned in life.
- Learning: the skill of earning knowledge is one that every successful business owner has. It is also a skill that they never stop developing.

To be successful in your entrepreneurial dreams you have to be able to learn from others. The best way to learn the skills of a successful business owner is to study the skills of successful entrepreneurs and then to grow those skills in yourself.

How Why I Started My Business
Although I have been involve in buisness since I was a teenager. I actuallly sponsored myself through collage by selling car accessories on campus to my professors and their friends. So, I have been in business long before I knew what entrepreneurship is all about.

In 2011 I had a shift in my life, and that led me to started asking lots of questions. As a result my entrepreneur mind got activated. But why should I go into active business and become an entrepreneur? For me I wanted to stop working for somebody and build a legacy for my children. My vision is to leave a business behind for my children and generations that would follow.

I knew I had to build something that is transferrable to my children as an inheritance. Working in another man's company will not be transferred to them. My ministry is non for profit, and that also would not be transferred to them. But I could build a business; established and successful - it can endure from generation to generation for my family to benefit from.

Each time I share this idea in conferences, seminar or worshop, I see more people open up to idea of starting a business, even if it is something small on the side, you never know where God can take it.

Chapter Two

DEVELOPING A POSITIVE ATTITUDE

Your mind is the single most important definer of success. If you're positive about your business, where it is headed and your role in the creation and growth of it then you're in a great place. From that place of positive emotion anything can and will happen. That being said, it can be difficult to sustain a positive attitude. Everyone has moment where negative thoughts, people, and emotions sneak in. The goal is to be able to recognize these moments, acknowledge them for what they are, and let them go. Here is how to develop and sustain a positive attitude.

Passion
Passion and a positive attitude are directly linked. When you have passion for your business everything else falls in line much

more easily. Unfortunately, you cannot develop passion for your business. You either have it or you do not. Hopefully, when you started your business it was something that you felt very strongly about.

If not, if you've never had passion for your business consider starting a business that you are passionate about. Learn from this and move forward.

Now, passion can wane. It can come and go. The secret to sustaining passion for your business is actually intricately linked with an entrepreneurial mind. When you're looking for ways to grow and improve your business, passion grows with the activity, the changes and the opportunities you pursue.

Create a Success Habit
When you are able to consistently set goals and achieve them, you'll create a pattern of success. Success of course feels great. It helps you stay focused on what you can do, what you do well, and where you want to go. That's the essence of a positive mind.

Not sure where to start? Create a realistic but motivating goal and a goal that you feel very good about. Create a series of smaller goals to help you achieve your big goal. Plan how you're going to achieve each smaller goal. As you succeed with each smaller goal, take a moment to celebrate the success.

Acknowledge, Assess, and Release

Doubts, fears and negative thought can sneak in. No one is positive all the time. When you have moments of doubt, fear and negative thoughts recognize the emotion. Assess where it is coming from and why it is occurring. It may take some time if you're prone to negative thoughts and limiting beliefs.

What's a limiting belief?

Here are a few common examples,

- This is never going to work.
- I am such a terrible _
- I'm bad with _
- The only way to succeed is with luck.
- I always mess this up.

If you frequently experience thoughts like

these then it is vitally important to spend some time refocusing your thoughts. Think about what you do well. Examine where the negative thoughts are coming from and why they occur. Assess whether they're really true and what you can do about them.

Positive Affirmations

We all struggle with limiting beliefs and doubts. You can turn these fears, limiting beliefs and doubts into positive affirmations. For example, I am bad at writing can turn into I am a good communicator. I know my strengths and weaknesses and am wise enough to delegate and focus on my strengths. Repeat the affirmation each time negativity seeps into your thoughts. Make a habit of repeating the positive affirmation regularly. Make it part of your inner dialogue.

Visualization

Visualization is a powerful tool. It not only helps you foresee potential obstacles to success, it helps you feel successful and positive about your actions. Visualization, like most things, is a skill. Some people are born with exceptional visualization skills; however most of us can use some improvement.

When you're beginning to use visualization, you will likely begin by simply seeing what is happening in your imagination. However, adding your senses will not only enhance the experience, it will amplify the results. Sight, touch, smell, taste and hearing can all be integrated into your visualizations.

Practice visualization. The better you become at visualization the faster you will achieve success. You'll be better able to tap into positive thoughts, feelings and a sense of success and achievement. When you're feeling negatively, sit down and visualize success. It will become part of your DNA if you embrace positive thoughts on such a deep level.

Surround Yourself with Positive People
The people in your life can play a very critical role in your attitude. Surrounded by negative people and naysayers? Consider asking them for support. Consider also finding a mentor, coach or mastermind group to help you stay focused and positive. Let go of the people in your life who cannot or will not support you.

Embrace those who support you and share the same outlook. That doesn't mean you surround yourself with yes men. You don't need people who simply agree with you. Instead look for those who are also positive, motivated and share the same vision.

A positive outlook and motivation are intricately linked. You cannot feel motivated if you also don't feel good about what you're doing and where you're going. In Chapter Two we'll take a closer look at how the two are connected and how together they affect every other aspect of your entrepreneurial mind.

Chapter Three

THE MOTIVATION EQUATION

Do you wake up each day excited to work on your business? Do you spend time thinking about your business even when you're not at work? For many, motivation is difficult to sustain. Some days are better than other. However, when you're truly excited about your business, and it becomes an active and positive part of your life, everything changes. When you wake up each day and you feel motivated and excited about your business, it opens the door for the other aspects of an entrepreneurial mind. You look for opportunities, you seize challenges, find creative solutions for problems and you effectively share your vision with others.

When you're not motivated it becomes difficult to do anything other than manage your business. And you're not a manager and you're an entrepreneur!

Let's take a look at a few key steps you can take to find motivation for your business. Note: If you can't summon any motivation for your present business, consider finding an idea that does inspire and motivate you.

Gratitude

Gratitude is the ability to recognize and appreciate what you have. It is also a practice. How often do you feel gratitude? Do you feel appreciative of:
- The things you have?
- The people in your life?
- Your daily experiences?

Gratitude accomplishes amazing things. It helps you stay positive and it has a dramatic affect on your motivation. Why? Because gratitude is something you want to feel more of and you want others to feel. It permeates your spirit and becomes part of who you are.

In order to benefit from gratitude it is important to make it a part of your life. Consider creating a habit of gratitude. Start saying, and feeling,

Thank you when you experience something wonderful or receive something in your life. Start acknowledging the things you are grateful for. You can journal or simply create a daily practice of mentally listing the things you're grateful for.

Focus On Your Strengths and Joyous and Fulfilling Activities.
- What do you love to do?
- What are you good at?
- Don't know?

Make a list. Start with the activities you love to do and the topics you're passionate about.

Then create a plan to integrate these joyous and fulfilling activities into your day. Make sure you do something you love each and every day. It is sure to get you out of bed in the morning and excited and motivated for your day.

Celebrate
Celebrate your successes. Each day, whatever you accomplish it doesn't matter if it is big or small, celebrate your successes. It'll add a smile to your face, a bounce to your step, and

it will help you stay motivated to achieve more success.

Get Inspired

One great way to stay inspired and motivated is to surround yourself with inspiration. So what inspires you? Music? Art? Books?
Create a home office that you enjoy spending time in. Surround yourself with the things you love. And of course, take the time to surround yourself with inspiring people.
It is hard to feel unmotivated with such greatness all around you.

Take Breaks

An annual vacation isn't enough. It is very important to your mental health and wellbeing to take breaks. Schedule daily breaks. Make sure to take time off weekly and monthly. And of course don't forget those annual vacations if that's part of your tradition.

How many scheduled breaks do you take? Even a few hours or a day or two can really make a difference. It gives you time to recharge and find that original source of inspiration and motivation.

Motivation can wane from day to day and even from task to task. However, being able to sustain motivation for your business is important. You want to feel excited about your business. It is the only way to really make it grow. Speaking of growth, the next step is all about tapping into your creative side and generating great, not to mention profitable, business ideas.

Chapter Four

HOW TO GENERATE A STEADY STREAM OF IDEAS AND TAPPING INTO YOUR CREATIVE SIDE

How innovative are you? Are you able to consistently practice creative brainstorming? Do you enjoy the process?

Many people don't consider themselves to be the Creative types yet everyone has the potential to be creative. Additionally, being creative doesn't mean you have to paint, write poetry or play a musical instrument. You can, sure, but it is not required.

Instead think of being creative as:
- Innovation
- Out of the box thinking
- Problem solving

Creative thinking means pondering the possibilities of what could be, without restrictions based on what is.

You might brainstorm:
- A new perspective on how to perform a task.
- A new way to market your business.
- A new partnership or joint venture.
- A new product or service.

How to Engage Your Creative Problem Solving Mind
1. Identify two or three problems your business is facing. They might be systems, strategies or even products or services.
2. Once you have your problems listed, brainstorm solutions. Write them down. Think about solutions without limiting yourself. Whenever a doubt surfaces about a potential solution push it aside.
3. Focus solely on brainstorming possibilities without restrictions or limitations. Push yourself to come up with potential solutions. This will really challenge you to get creative with your answers.
4. Consider doing something routine while

you're brainstorming. For example, toss a ball from hand to hand. Chop vegetables or some other activity that requires eye and hand coordination. Studies have shown that this practice opens up another area of your brain.

It is why great ideas come to us when we're driving, exercising, praying and other routine activities. Try it if you have trouble tapping into your creative side.

Add creative brainstorming sessions into your regular work week. Make it part of your life as an entrepreneur. It is a part of your work week you'll begin to look forward to and it'll generate amazing results.

The Idea Equation
IE = Subject + Problem / Benefit + Business model

#1 Subject
- Who is benefiting from your idea?
- It could be a group of people, other businesses, etc.
- Always pick a specific group.

#2 **Problems/Benefits**
- Problems: You identify something people are struggling with, a pain point, and you make a solution to fix it.
- Benefits: Find some value that you can add; people will pay to enjoy it.

#3 **Business Model**
- The way in which you will address the problem and get your solution to the customer.
- Always have more business models just in case the first one doesn't work.

In addition to brainstorming ideas and opportunities it is important to be aware of the opportunities already present in your life. Chapter Five talks about how to be more open and aware of opportunities.

Chapter Five

HOW TO BE MORE OPEN AND AWARE OF OPPORTUNITIES

Every day new opportunities come your way. The problem is that most people don't recognize them. And those that do recognize the opportunity let fear, doubt and negativity get in the way of taking action.

This is why so many of these entrepreneurial mind elements are important. Right away you can see that staying positive helps you take action and recognize opportunities. They're all linked together and strengthen one and you strengthen them all.

There are essentially five steps to be more open to opportunities that come your way.

Step #1 Stay Positive

If you're feeling negative then your head is down and you're focusing on limitations. It is the opposite of what you want to do. Stay positive and expect good things. You'll recognize them when they come your way. Refer back to Chapter One on how to get and stay positive.

Step #2 Listen

There is a lot going on in your community, both online and off. Listen to what your community is saying. Pay attention to leaders in your industry. Listen to your customers and listen to those around you.

Sometimes listening is difficult. We get involved in talking, sharing and making a great impression. Try listening to those around you instead of talking and see what happens.

Step #3 Be Open Minded

It is easy to shut the door on an opportunity. It takes an open mind to consider all the possibilities that come your way. An open mind often requires courage and a positive attitude and two other qualities of an entrepreneurial mind.

Step #4 Take Inspired Action

You might be the kind of person that regularly recognizes opportunities. However, do you then take action on those that come your way? Action doesnít mean diving headlong into a new commitment. Instead, action might be as simple as brainstorming ideas related to the opportunity or researching it further.

It is not enough to acknowledge an opportunity. You want to seize the moment and take inspired action. It ís one of the core components of an entrepreneurial mind. See an opportunity and take action!

Step #5 Look for Opportunities

Finally, and this is an integral part of the Creative Thinking attribute that has already been discussed, start looking for opportunities. It is not enough to wait for them to come your way. Start looking for opportunities or making them for yourself.

Now, we just talked about taking inspired action. That can be difficult if you're not taking advantage of all your resources. You can't do everything yourself!

Listening to an Opportunity Is Not Enough; You Have to Put It into Action

When you work for someone it makes it more easy for you, typically they take all the risk, guide you, inform you what to do and how to do but when you choose to start your own business it's totally a new game. The main part to starting your own business is that you need to take action, action and action.

You should not only plan on what to do, when to do and how to do but also implement the plan you have made. As it's your business you only have to take action, no one else will do the initiative.

One of the most import reasons of people not getting success is lack of hard work, or commitments to themselves. You need to execute your plan instantly. Merely thinking about the opportunity at the drop of a hat and trying to implement it isn't going to take you anywhere.

If you work hard and execute your plans as per plan, you will surely get rewards which you expected and many times much more than expected.

There is a saying that action speaks louder than words. So put your plans into action and see how it gives you returns. You don't get anything just by speaking it out; you need to actually do that. It's not difficult to be a go getter or put your plans into action. Just be confident, be committed to yourself and you will see the results.

There is unlimited potential for hardworking people and for those who put their plans in action and not just listen to an opportunity.

Chapter Six

BE VERY COMPETITIVE

Being competitive is defined as characterized by competition. Competition is the rivalry among sellers trying to achieve such goals as increasing profits, market share, and sales volume by varying the elements of the marketing mix such as prices, products, distribution, and advertisement.

Competitive Strategy

A very important factor for ambitious entrepreneurs, competitive strategy is defined as the long term plan of a particular company in order to gain competitive advantage over its competitors in the industry. It is directed at creating defensive spots in an industry and producing a superior return on Investments.

Questions to be kept in mind
- Who are your competitors?
- What products or services do they sell?
- What is each competitor's market share?
- What are their past strategies?
- What are their current strategies?
- What type of media are used to market their products or services?
- How many hours per week do they purchase to advertise through the media used in this market?
- What are each competitor's strengths and weaknesses?
- What potential threats do your competitors pose?
- What potential opportunities do they make available for you?

Fail proof ways to have competitive advantage

Having competitive advantage over one's competitors is very important for a business to succeed. This is especially more important for entrepreneur who are just starting out.

Following are a few ways aspiring entrepreneurs can gain that advantage.

1. Placing is better than seeking

Most businesses are looking for prospects, clients and customers. This never-ending process will definitely be a cause of a burn out, eventually. Burn out is always tough to scale. An easier way to approach your business is to position yourself as the leading authority, expert, specialist or trusted advisor on your subject. This requires strategic and deliberate action, but you shall reap exponential rewards. When you're perceived as the authority figure and an expert, people will start coming to you. Be exclusive, and make it an honor to work with you.

2. Plans fail, movements don't

Reposition your business and make sure it's about something. The entrepreneurs on a mission bigger than themselves are always attracting top tier talent. Life becomes much more fulfilling when you become involved in a movement or a cause greater than yourself.

3. Stand on the shoulders of giants

You don't need to reinvent the apple firm, and you really don't need to figure everything out yourself. Search for something that is already working and make it better. A bird cannot become a fish, so just be the best bird you can be.

A clever person learns from their mistakes, as all successful people do, but those wanting world-class results learn from other people's mistakes so they can shorten their learning curve, and not waste as much time.

4. Create raging fans and advocates
Business is the management of promises and if you can consistently deliver and keep promises for all your customers, you are ahead of the game. It's much more expensive to get a new customer than it is to take care of the ones you have.

The purpose of business is to create frantic fans and advocates, who will go out of their way to promote what you do. Not because you asked them, but because they want to. Outstanding client support and service is affected by every person in your organization. You must create a culture where people are passionate.

Chapter Seven

TAKE ADVANTAGE OF YOUR RESOURCES

Entrepreneurs know two very important things.
1. They know they cannot, and should not, do it all.
2. They know that others can and are willing to help - they use their resources

What Are Your Resources?

Take a look around you and make a list of your resources. Consider:
- The people in your life.
- The people you can bring into your life (for example, contractors, consultants and mentors).
- The technology in your life.
- The technology you can bring into your life.

- Your skills, knowledge and abilities.
- The skills, knowledge and abilities of others.
- Financial assets.

The list could go on and on because resources are all around you. Unfortunately, many business owners get into the mind that they have to do it all. They have to be the manager, salesperson, customer service department, financial officer, and so on. It leaves very little, if any, time for the entrepreneur.

If you're always taking care of the business, how do you grow it? Easy and You grow it by taking advantage of your resources.

Step #1 Identify Your Resources.
Who and what do you have in your life right now that can help you with your business? For example, do you have technology that you're not taking advantage of that can simplify some of your systems? Do you know a bookkeeper that could manage your accounting so you don't have to?

Step #2 Identify Where You Need Help Right Now

Spend some time looking at where you need help. What tasks are you managing that:
- Take up too much time
- Aren't enjoyable
- Don't match your skill set
- Don't result in direct profits

These are prime opportunities to take advantage of your resources. Additionally, if you don't have a resource to solve a problem go out and get one.

For example, if you need someone to take over your bookkeeping but you don't know a bookkeeper then hire a bookkeeper. Your time is too valuable to spend it on tasks than manage your business. You need time to be the entrepreneur.

Step #3 Acknowledge Future Opportunities as Potential Resources

You just never know when you're going to be presented with a potential solution. And these solutions often pop up when you don't need them.

For example, you're in line at the grocery store and you start a conversation with the person in line ahead of you. You quickly learn that he or she is a graphic designer. You don't have a need for a graphic designer so you nod politely.

A month later you need a graphic designer. Oh, if only you'd taken the business card of the person in line at the grocery store!

You will find potential resources through:
1. Networking and online and offline
2. Continuous learning
3. Sharing your vision with others. People will connect with it and show you how they can help.

Your resources are all around you. You simply have to recognize them and put them to good use. Don't neglect this very profitable and effective attribute of an entrepreneurial mind. It'll help you with the attribute we talk about in the next chapter.

Chapter Eight

RESILIENCE IN ENTREPRENEUR

To be a successful entrepreneur you need to develop resilience. Resilience can defined as the capacity to recover quickly from the difficulties and hurdles one faces. These hurdles and difficulties can be very frustrating at times. The key is to bounce back and not let the frustration grow.

Resilience is a term that has different meanings to different people. For a group of Psychologists the word resilience means to get back to normal routine after being hit with shocks or traumatic events. However, in the business community, resilience refers to the continuation of producing value and productivity in the face of man-made or natural disasters.

Secret To Entrepreneur's Resilient Factors

According to some experts, such as Dennis McCormack and a few others, there are a few key factors of resilience and human behavior that every entrepreneur should live by. Make these factors your rules before determined entrepreneurs start.

1. Sustain vigorous optimism

Optimistic people have a specific mindset. They have trained their minds to expect the best outcome from every situation. This gives entrepreneurs the ability to pivot from a failing approach. This also makes them implement actions which are to increase the success rate. The key to building active optimism is to simply observe how others were successful in similar situations. Thinking of how a certain personality would handle a similar situation and also believing you can do the same.

2. Take decisive action

An entrepreneurs must have the courage to make decisions and then act on them. Decisiveness alleviates harsh conditions, helps you rebound, take charge, and encourages growth. In order to become decisive one must eliminate fears, phobias, procrastination, and the wish to please everyone. Practice making decisions as a positive learning experience. One thing to be kept in mind is an active decision is better than no decision in a time of difficulty.

3. A good moral compass

Once in awhile everyone needs a guiding light, especially when hard times strike. Let a good moral compass be your guide. Honesty, integrity, fidelity, and ethical behavior are the four major points that work best not only in business but in personal life. Strengthen your moral compass by setting honorable objectives, keying off the norm of inspiring peers, practicing self-control, and celebrating every time you are successful.

4. Demonstrate persistent tenacity and determination

This is one very important factor. For one thing, entrepreneurship is not an easy task. You might fall down a few times but each time you need to pull yourself back up, dust off the failure and get back on the horse. Decide that giving up is simply not an option. Know that tenacity is self-sustaining when determined actions are rewarded. Find tenacious idols, and garner the support of peers and friends. Great entrepreneurs become tenaciously rebellious when told they cannot succeed. Then they get it done!

5. Gain strength from social support
In business, this means that the people you. So, surround yourself with team members, advisors, investors, partners, and peers. Like any other part of your life, in order to succeed, avoid toxic and negative people like the plague. Practice active listening and show appreciation. Interpersonal support is thought to be the best driver of human resilience.

Chapter Nine

HOW TO WEAR THE ENTREPRENEURIAL HAT (YOU'RE MORE THAN A MANAGER)

Presumably you started your business for a number of reasons. Maybe you were inspired to make a positive change in the world. Maybe you wanted to share your knowledge, skills or experience with others.

Maybe you simply wanted to have the freedom to be your own boss and make your own decisions. Chances are you didn't want to become a manager. Yet if you're spending your days managing:
- Email
- Customer service
- Fulfillment and delivery

- Bookkeeping
- Affiliates
- Autoresponders
- Project management

And much more, then you definitely don't have enough time to be an entrepreneur. You don't have the time you need to innovate, plan and take inspired action.

How to Wear the Entrepreneurial Hat
Presumably you won't be able to outsource, delegate and automate everything for your business. There will still be some managerial tasks you have to take on. There will still be many tasks you need to or want to handle that are not entrepreneurial in nature. It is your company and you're the person who gets to make the rule.

That being said it is very important to take the manager and task manager hat off on a regular basis and focus on being the entrepreneur. What does that mean? It means spending time brainstorming, innovating, creating and developing new business ideas and systems. For example, the owner of a coaching business spends a lot of time actually coaching clients. It is still important to spend time to spend time each week creating systems, products and services that benefit their audience. They might create information products to generate passive income or brainstorm ways to offer more value to their coaching clients.

Here is how to make sure you consistently put on the Entrepreneurial Hat.

Step One: Set Time Aside To Brainstorm and Plan
Planning is an important part of being a business owner. Consider setting time aside each week to plan your business. A bare minimum is once monthly. However, the more often you plan, the more comfortable you'll be with the process.

Step Two: Delegate Responsibility
Outsourcing has already been mentioned. However, you can also partner, hire employees and embrace the idea of interns. Each new person you bring on your team plays an important role in your business. Let them play that role. Delegate responsibility so you have

time to be the entrepreneur and so you have time to plan and grow your business.

Step Three: Know your Strengths and Weaknesses
We'll talk about this in Chapter Eleven but for now know that it ís important when you're planning how to grow your business and profits that you're keenly aware of your strengths and weaknesses. This will help you plan your role in any new system, product or service you create. It'll also help you decide who to delegate or outsource tasks to.

It ís important to acknowledge your role and responsibility for growing your business. That means setting time aside to make it happen. It also means knowing your strengths and weaknesses and then building a team of people to help you reach your goals. In order to do that you want to be able to share and communicate your vision.

Chapter Ten

HOW TO SHARE YOUR BUSINESS VISION

Entrepreneurs are visionaries. They dream of the possibilities and then take action to make it happen. That means you want to be able to effectively communicate your dream or vision. Here is how:

Create a Vision Statement
Do you have a vision statement? If not, spend some time defining exactly what you want your business to become.

Your vision statement answers the question, Where do I want this business to go? What do I want this business to be?

Here is an example of a vision statement. Five years from now, my company will have annual revenues of over $250,000 by consistently providing timely, reasonably priced repair and coaching services.

Of course the statement could have read to indicate a goal of reaching 1000 clients or broadening services to include information products.

The vision statement is guided by you and what you want for your future and the future of your business. It doesn't have to be money focused.

If you don't have a vision for your business start creating it. Write it down and keep it somewhere handy. This will make it easier for you to access when you're making business decisions and it'll make it easier to communicate your vision.

Aim High, like the Air Force

Do you know what you're capable of? You might think you do, but for most people what they can actually achieve is quite different than what they think they can achieve. You have probably heard the axiom: whether you think you can or you can't, you're right. People have set world records in athletic events, and experts have deemed some of them the fastest or best the human body is capable of, and then someone from a remote part of the world didn't get the memo that there was a limit as to what the human body was capable of until after they'd already broken the record.

Set your goals higher than you think you can achieve. Of course, don't set them outrageously high to the point where they're unrealistic, but set them higher than you think you're probably capable of.

For example, our previous goal of earning an extra $10,000 in 12 months is pretty reasonable and probably achievable depending on what you do to make it happen. If your goal is to make $100,000 over the next 12 months, that's pretty unrealistic. But what if your goal was to make an extra $15,000 in 12 months? You might think that you're only capable of making an extra $10,000 but by setting the go higher you have something to aim for, and suppose you only make $12,000; that's still $2000 more than your original goal.

Putting Goals into Action

You want to make a list of around five goals to start with. The number is not important; it is arbitrary. What is important is that you create enough goals that will allow you to accomplish something substantial in the next 12 months, or five years, or whatever your timeframe is, and not so many goals that you have no chance of achieving them all. Then, for each goal, you're going to make a plan of action. Earlier we used the analogy of driving a car to a vacation destination. Your plan of action is that car; it is the vehicle that is going to take you all the way to the end where your success waits.

Your plan of action is going to take you from where you are now all the way to the end result, which is your goal. It is going to include milestones, or places that you stop along the way to check your progress as well as specific small goals that you'll need to achieve to get to the big goal. It is sort of like playing a videogame – you have to beat all of the easy monsters before you get to the big boss at the end of the level. If your goal is to make an extra $10,000 in the next 12 months then you need to know what specific things you need to do to make that happen. Are you planning to start an online store? Are you making investments? Whatever your method is, you'll have specific things that you need to accomplish, and that makes up the framework for your plan of action.

Once you have a vision statement, the first step to communicating it is to be passionate about it. Are you excited about where your business is going and what the future has to offer?

So how do you consistently communicate your vision?

- Integrate it into your decision making process. For example, if you are presented with an opportunity ask yourself if it supports your vision.
- Find like minded people through networking.
- Hire and work with like minded people who understand your vision.
- Embrace your vision in your marketing and communications as well as your

sales, fulfillment and customer service department and make it an integral part of your business.

Chapter Eleven

HOW TO BE A PROBLEM SOLVER

The foundation of every business is that it solves a problem for their customers. It doesn't matter what business model or niche you're in as a business owner you are a problem solver. A personal trainer helps people solve the problem of their health and fitness. A cell phone store solves the problem of communication.

In order to grow your business you want to continue to identify the problems your audience and customers are experiencing and solve them with products, services and improved systems.

You are therefore a problem solver. A problem

solver is also an innovator and you come up with innovative solutions to problems. (Aka a Creative Problem Solver.)

One of the most difficult aspects of the entrepreneurial mind is recognizing innovative opportunities and becoming a creative problem solver.

Peter Drucker, in his book Innovation and Entrepreneurship, Practices and Principles, lists several potential sources for innovative opportunity including:

1. Process Need
Process Need is the need for a solution which arises from a process. For example, you're cutting an apple and you want an easier way to remove the skin. Ah-ha! The apple peeler is invented.

2. Industry Changes
Any new change to your industry provides new problems and new opportunities. Social media managers are an example of an industry created to solve the problem for an entirely new industry.

3. Demographics

As characteristics of the human population change so do the needs. For example, more self employed individuals means a demand for individual health insurance.

4. Changes in Perception

Perceptions change as cultures change. The green movement is a classic example of a change in perception. It has presented many new business opportunities and problems to solve. For example, green light bulbs.

5. New Knowledge

As we learn new things, new needs and demands are created. For example, you learn that grape seeds help with weight loss, suddenly there is a need for grape seed extract and supplements. Innovative opportunity is all around you. The trick is to recognize it. Thinking about innovative opportunities based on the above criteria may help you begin to develop this skill.

Becoming an Innovator and Problem Solver

It is really a matter of recognizing opportunities

and we've already discussed how to accomplish that. Next, create a process whereby you are able to document ideas as they come to you. It may involve carrying around a small notebook and pen (or it may involve simply dictating your ideas into your phone or mobile device.

Create a habit of recording your ideas. The more you record them as they come to you, the more ideas will freely flow.

Chapter Twelve

ENTREPRENEURIAL MIND MEANS BEING WILLING TO TAKE RISKS

Chances are, if you own a business, you're at least willing to take some risk. Entrepreneurs aren't careless. They know the difference between apparent and actual risk. They take what is often called calculated risk.

Calculated risk is risk that has been considered carefully. It is not without the potential for failure but you have carefully weighed the pros and the cons and decided to go ahead. The difference between an entrepreneur and most other people is that they're willing to take much more risk than others.

In fact, many entrepreneurs don't really consider the risks associated with failure or ridicule. These are two risks that stop most people in their tracks.

They're often not concerned about financial risk either. If you have a dream and you're passionate about it, the only risk to you is not seeing your dream become a reality and that is an entrepreneurial mind.

Risk Assessment - What Are You Afraid Of?

Not all fears are created equal. Fearing for your life is much different than fearing ridicule.

The body has a similar adrenaline response but the actual outcomes are very different. Fear ridicule and you may miss out on owning your dream business. Fear for your life and you stay alive.

An entrepreneur assesses their fears from a place of logic. They ask themselves, What do I really have to lose?

Once you know the worst, you can prepare for the best. You can then set aside your fear or overcome it. Our logical minds can be both a hindrance and a help and the key is to use it to your advantage.

Embrace the entrepreneurial mind and learn to recognize when your thoughts are limiting your success.

Chapter Thirteen

ENTREPRENEURS ALWAYS LEARN AND IMPROVE

Entrepreneurs are motivated, right? We've already covered that. They're motivated to:
- Grow their business
- Make money
- Help people
- Work less and earn more
- Provide value

They're also motivated to learn, grow and improve themselves. Why? Because self improvement and education helps them stay on the cutting edge of their business, offer more value to their customers, brainstorm and innovate new solutions, and ultimately make more money. Continued learning helps you also gain exposure to new people, thoughts, ideas, practices, philosophies, and opportunities.

Self improvement also helps you hone your entrepreneurial strengths. It helps you improve yourself. It also helps you adapt to new changes and opportunities quickly.

But how do you fit continued learning into your already busy life? Create a goal, a plan and a strategy for success of course!
- Read blogs and industry magazines and use technology to deliver information to a reader or your email.
- Network online.
- Join a mastermind group.
- Attend classes, seminars and workshops.
- Read industry books and business books.

You should never stop learning. No matter how much you know, there is always room for more information. Just as science discovers that the more that we figure out about the world around us in the universe, the more we realize that we don't know; It works the same way with your learning as well. Spend a little time each and every day learning something new that is going to help you.

You could read a motivational book. There are many different ones out there that are geared towards entrepreneurs and are written to give great advice from experts who actually have made a success out of entrepreneurship.

You can find them at your local library or online in digital format. Books by Anthony Robbins, Stephen R. Covey, Dale Carnegie and Napoleon Hill are all great reads if you're trying to motivate yourself and become more successful. There are many other places that you can find motivation. Go on YouTube during your free time and look for motivational videos if that's more your style or you could even correspond via email with someone who is more successful than you, who could be your mentor of sorts.

No matter how you get information, the point is, to keep learning and to devote some time each day to that learning. You don't even necessarily have to read motivational or self-help books. You could do something that improves yourself like learning a new language or teaching yourself a new skill, or by studying a subject that you been interested in, relating to your business.

Consider the following goal and to attend one workshop, seminar or online class each quarter. Subscribe to 10 of the top industry blogs and read them weekly. Join a mastermind group or find a mentor/coach and to read one industry book each quarter.

Continued learning and self improvement also helps you increase your strengths and manage your weaknesses. Of course, first you need to know what they are. On to Chapter Eleven!

Chapter Fourteen

ENTREPRENEURS KNOW THEIR STRENGTHS AND WEAKNESSES

Do you know what you're good at? Do you know where you need help in your business? This is truly important information. It takes a strong person to acknowledge their weaknesses and seek help for them.

For example, as a business owner maybe you're great at writing sales copy but not so skilled with the day to day content writing. Maybe your voice comes across as too salesy or forced and instead you want to be friendly and informative.

Instead of spending countless hours trying to improve your writing skills it might make more sense to find help in the form of a ghostwriter.

Entrepreneurs know that they cannot be good at everything and that it doesn't make sense for them to. Focus on your strengths. That is where the money and the satisfaction are. And find ways to manage or compensate for your weaknesses.

Hire experts. Create systems that don't require you to perform in your weak areas.
Improve your skills when and if it makes sense. For example if you want to be a better content writer or you simply cannot afford to hire someone to write all your content then it makes sense to work on improving your skills.

Sit down and document your strengths and weaknesses. Then create systems and solutions that work for you and your business goals.

Especially, you're going to make a list of things the entrepreneurs have to have in order to be successful. These can be both wide and specific depending on what your particular goals are. For example, they need to be good at whatever industry they are in and the are probably also going to want to be skilled in things like social networks, choosing products, building business relationships and marketing.

You're going to want to be as specific as you possibly can because at the end were going to compare the two lists and try to find how many strengths you have already that can help you be successful. The more things you list, the more things that you're going to discover are actually true about yourself. This exercise isn't actually about finding all of the qualities that entrepreneurs need to succeed; it is about realizing that you already have the attributes that it takes to be successful. You do have the attributes that it takes to be successful. This is readily apparent, because you're reading this book. People that are interested in success or aren't motivated to better themselves and reach their goals don't read books on success. In fact, they tend to avoid the subject as much as possible because it reminds them of their failures.

Here are some of the more apparent attributes just to get you started:
- Determination: you have the idea or attitude that you are going to succeed no matter what, no matter who stands in

your way and no matter what obstacles you encounter.

- A Passion for Entrepreneurship: if you aren't passionate about working for yourself and owning your own business, it can be almost impossible for you to be successful at it.

- Optimism: you are optimistic about the future. You believe that good things are in store for you and your outlook is almost always a glass half-full kind of mind.

- Patience: you are willing to work over a long period of time to get the results that you want. You're not going to give up if it doesn't happen quickly.

- Reliable: you will be able to handle the responsibility of being an entrepreneur. You have a reputation for being reliable so people are willing to work with you.

Finally, because all work and no play really does lead to disaster, the final chapter takes a look at living a balanced life.

Chapter Fifteen

LIVING THE ENTREPRENEUR LIFESTYLE

There are plenty of benefits to living the entrepreneur lifestyle. For many entrepreneurs this lifestyle equals freedom, purpose and enjoyment. It also means hard work and never ending motivation. The successful entrepreneur lives for their work. This doesn't mean that their job is the only thing in their life- it means that their work is their life's passion. Could you imagine waking up every day to go to a job that you love and cannot wait to do? This is the lifestyle of the successful entrepreneur and is why it is so vitally important for you to choose something that you are truly passionate about.

The entrepreneur's lifestyle is also one of the main reasons why you will want to undergo this amazing transformation. It is why you want to do something different and more meaningful with your life. This is the different choice. It is not the 'rat race' or the 'daily grind'. It is not 'working for the man'. It is working for yourself, by yourself and for what you appreciate the most in life. It is a life choice.

Enjoying Your Success
Hopefully you will have what it takes to become a truly successful entrepreneur and will be able to push yourself to accomplish everything it takes to be successful. If you are able to accomplish these feats you will be able to experience what few other people in this world will be able to feel- the ability to enjoy your success in life.

Almost all forms of success bring the pleasure and pride of achievement with them, but few will taste as sweet as success that is self-made. It is truly an amazing thing to be able to look at your successful life, which includes your passion, your dream, your ability to live the kind of life you want and your financial security, and know that it was you who achieved it! So few people have only themselves to thank for the amazing life they live. This feeling is worth more than any money or material possessions you can think of. It is a feeling that can only be experienced through the success of entrepreneurship.

The purpose behind becoming an entrepreneur is to take the time to truly stop and enjoy your success. If not, what is the point of all of your hard work?

All work and no play is a surefire way to burn out, lose motivation and energy for your business. If you spend all of your time and energy building your business and don't spend any time on yourself, your friends, your family and the other aspects of your personal life you are in danger. There is the very real risk that you'll burn out, or worse and lose your personal life.

No one can tell you how to define success. You know what success means to you. And no one can tell you how to define a balanced life. You know what balance means to you.

Maybe balance means you work three weeks

and then take a week off. Or balance might mean you work in the mornings and take the afternoons off. Or maybe the standard five day work week with two weeksí vacation is just fine.

The important thing to know is that you do need to take time off. You do need to focus on other things some times.

- How do you know if you're living a balanced life? It is pretty easy actually.
- Do you wake up feeling motivated and enthusiastic about your day? Are you able to focus on your tasks?
- Do you feel creative and inspired?

If the answer is yes to all three then you're probably doing just fine. If you answer no to any of the questions at any time then you need a break.

Instead of waiting for that no answer and feelings of motivation to wane, plan for a balanced life. Schedule time off and figure out what you need both personally and professionally.

When you live a balanced life it is easy to unleash your inner entrepreneur. It is easy to embrace your entrepreneurial mind.

Conclusion

At the core of any entrepreneur is someone who is so excited and passionate about their business that they're ready and willing and able to take risks. They're positive about the direction they're headed and they're willing to bring others along for the ride and in fact they'd prefer it that way.

So if you think you have what it takes to take on the challenge and develop an entrepreneurial mind, you should immediately begin the process of doing so. The good news is that there are numerous tools available to help you along the way. From mastering the basic skills and personality traits of successful business owners to learning the finer points of marketing a company, there are hundreds of thousands of learning tools out there to help you achieve your goals. If you are willing to learn the knowledge it will be easily presented to you.

The best advice anyone can give an aspiring entrepreneur is to take advantage of the informational world we live in and to learn as much as you can whenever you can. Smart people take every advantage they can find, and the vast amounts of knowledge available is certainly a considerable advantage. Learn what you need to know to become a successful entrepreneur and then create a mind within yourself that allows you to make the appropriate changes to your physical and mental self. There is nothing you cannot do if you set your mind to it!

It is about being more than a business owner and you're a problem solver and a creator. You're an entrepreneur!

BONUS

SETTING YOUR BUSINESS GOALS

Often Entrepreneurs spend too much time asking the question, "What's the next big thing?".

Unfortunately, they rarely ask the correct question which is "What do I want out of my next venture?"

Use this worksheet to set your goals and expectations. Once you know what you want, you'll know what to shoot for. Knowing what you need is half the battle.

This exercise will practically put you in the right path as well motivate you to take necessary actions toward achieving your business success.

How big do you want your next business to be?

Example answers:
- As big as possible
- 100+ employees
- 50 employees Small crew of <10
- Myself + 2-3 people
- Just me

Your answer:

How long are you willing to work on this next business?

Example answers:
- Forever
- As long as it takes
- 10 years+
- 5-7 years
- 2-4 years
- 1-2 years
- < 1 year

Your Answer:

How much money will the business need to make, to be satisfied?

Example answers:
- Nothing
- 1k a month
- 3k a month
- Minimum 5k a month
- 5 – 10k a month
- I want to make millions

Your answer:

How many hours per week are you willing to work on this business?

Example answers:
- As needed
- 5 hours
- 10-15 hours
- 25 hours
- 2-4 years
- 1-2 years
- < 1 year

Your Answer:

How long could you wait for this business to become profitable?

Example answers:
- Forever
- As long as it takes
- 1 month
- 2-3 months
- 3-6 months
- 1 year
- 2 years

Your answer:

How much of your resources are you willing to commit?

Example answers:
- Everything I have + loans if needed
- Everything I have
- <$20,000
- <$10,000
- <$1,000
- $100
- Just my time

Your answer:

NOTE

NOTE

NOTE

NOTE

NOTE

NOTE

www.ingramcontent.com/pod-product-compliance
Lightning Source LLC
Chambersburg PA
CBHW070650050426
42451CB00008B/328